A souvenir guide

Avebury Manor

Wiltshire

C000071716

National Trust

A Classic English Manor House

Amid one of the greatest surviving concentrations of Neolithic and Bronze Age monuments in Western Europe, and close to the largest stone circle in the world, lies this classic English manor house.

The earliest surviving part of Avebury Manor appears to have been built by a Tudor courtier, probably in the 1550s, on the site of a twelfth-century Benedictine priory. Successive families acquired and enlarged the building; the wealthier ones added another wing, while the socially ambitious may have entertained a passing monarch. The manor was the last home of a former Governor of Jamaica, but during the nineteenth century it housed generations of hard-working tenant farmers. A married couple, both lovers of traditional buildings, bought and painstakingly restored Avebury Manor in 1907, but financial worries forced them to sell their beloved home.

Above Avebury from the south

A marmalade millionaire

Between the wars it was home to Alexander Keiller, a millionaire marmalade magnate and keen archaeologist, whose hobbies ranged from studying witchcraft to collecting cow creamers. He used it as a base for his excavations of the neighbouring prehistoric site, much of which he also owned, and which he later sold to the National Trust. After his sale of Avebury Manor in 1955, it changed hands several times. The last private owner opened the site as a Tudor-themed attraction, but was declared bankrupt, and in 1991 the National Trust bought the house from the Official Receivers. It was virtually devoid of any original contents, so it was leased to private tenants, with limited public opening.

Memories of England

'More than once I have taken visitors from overseas to Avebury … and I have said, "Do please let this one scene fasten on your memory. Whatever memories of England you carry away, let this be uppermost. For this, to me, is England."'

R.C. Hutchinson, novelist

Right Alexander Keiller, who excavated Avebury in the 1930s

The manor reborn

When the tenancy ended in 2009, we decided to increase public access to the house. Coincidentally, the BBC was searching for an empty historic house which could be researched, furnished and decorated appropriately, as the basis for a documentary series. Avebury Manor, almost unfurnished but redolent of its venerable past, was the ideal setting for the four-part TV series *The Manor Reborn*, broadcast in November–December 2011.

The complex collaboration between historical experts, National Trust staff, and the Russell Sage Studio involved skilled craftspeople, volunteers and artists. The imaginative plan was to decorate the rooms to reflect key moments in its history, linked to the real stories of the house and its occupants. The contents had been sold in 1902, but period furniture and textiles had been used here during the following century. It was agreed that traditionally-made replica pieces could be installed, as long as the fabric of the building was not damaged in any way. Through the robust, bespoke artefacts and furnishings, combined with 'sacrificial' authentic objects, you are now encouraged to explore the house in a new way.

Why don't you …?

- *Stretch out in the armchairs*
- *Fiddle with the kitchen gadgets*
- *Play snooker*
- *Try out the beds*
- *Imagine life as a Tudor courtier, a Stuart queen, a millionaire playboy or a kitchenmaid*

The Families of Avebury

The Dunch family

William Dunch (*c.*1508–97) rose from obscurity, entered the Royal Household, and served two kings and two queens. He side-stepped the power struggles and religious turmoil of the Tudor Court, though he spent time in prison in 1549. He was an Auditor of the Royal Mint, and High Sheriff of Berkshire, the official representative of Queen Elizabeth.

The builder of the house
In 1551 William Dunch bought the Avebury estate for £2,000 from William Sharington, who had been implicated in a plot against Edward VI and was lucky to escape execution. Dunch had married in 1547 and over the following years he acquired considerable property and appears to have built the present house. His principal home was at Little Wittenham, Oxfordshire, which, like Avebury, was notable for its prehistoric remains.

A tactful courtier
When he died, aged 89, in 1597, William's will declared his allegiance to Queen Elizabeth, describing himself as '…a sworne servant to her most noble father & to her brother and sister and also to herself…', and this tactful courtier also left his last monarch a bequest: 'one ringe with a diamond or peece of plate of the worth and value of fortie pounds'.

Top **William Sharington, who sold Avebury to William Dunch**

Above **The memorial of William and Mary Dunch in Little Wittenham church in Oxfordshire**

The Mervyns

Walter Dunch, the son of William and Mary Dunch, took over the Avebury estate in the early 1580s around the time of his marriage. He died in 1594, leaving a widow, Deborah, and five children. A dispute arose between Deborah and a neighbour, Richard Truslowe of Truslowe Manor, over the ownership of the stone pigeon house (the dovecote in the present farmyard).

By law, only a Lord of the Manor was entitled to keep pigeons, and Richard was claiming the prestigious title. Deborah appears to have appealed to the influential Sir James Mervyn, MP and High Sheriff of Wiltshire, whom she married in 1597 or 1598. Together they won the case.

A pioneer colony

One of the Dunches' daughters, Lady Deborah Moody, became an Anabaptist, believing that children should not be baptised as Christians until maturity. To avoid persecution, Deborah emigrated to Massachusetts in the 1630s, when she was around 50 years old. Even the devout English Puritan settlers of North America found Deborah's convictions extreme and excommunicated her, so she joined the Dutch colony. In 1645 the Dutch granted her and her associates permission to found a town, Gravesend, in what is now Brooklyn, New York. Deborah died in the late 1650s, in her 70s. Meanwhile her brother, William, had inherited Avebury Manor, but in 1640 sold it to Sir John Stawell. It was bought in 1694 by Sir Richard Holford, Master in Chancery, for £7,500.

Left The Avebury dovecote was at the centre of a dispute between Sir James Mervyn and Richard Truslowe, who lived nearby

Far left The plasterwork ceiling in the Tudor Parlour may have been put up by the Mervyns

A fashionable frontispiece

Sir James and Deborah Mervyn extended the house by adding a substantial hall and service rooms, with a suite of rooms above. The Mervyns put in a handsome studded oak front door, and a porch in the Renaissance style, topped with their joined initials, MID, standing for 'Mervyn, James and Deborah', and the date, 1601.

The Holfords

Wealthy barrister Sir Richard Holford already owned Westonbirt in Gloucestershire, but following his third marriage, to a Miss Susanna Trotman, he bought Avebury Manor for her and their future children as part of the marriage settlement.

Susanna left £200 in her will to provide instruction for the poor children of Avebury. Richard and Susanna's only surviving child, Samuel, died in 1730, so the property passed to a grandson of Sir Richard's second marriage. His grandson, also Richard, converted the Great Hall into a classical dining room, and raised the roof of the chamber above it. Richard's brother Stayner inherited in 1742, and he lived at Avebury with his half-brother Arthur Jones, until his death in 1767. Arthur agonised about the fate of Avebury Manor for the next 22 years, finally settling the property on his niece Anne Williamson and her husband. She complied with his wishes that following his death (which occurred in 1789) his coffin should be left open for a week; fear of being accidentally buried alive was rife at this time.

A royal visit

'Thursday ye 13 [August 1712] about 10 we came to Sir Ric. Holford's house in Avebery it is a noble large antient seat built with whit larg stone, it did belong to Lord Stoil, the late noble Lord Stoil was born there and our Queen Ann dined there…'

John Saunders (a servant of Lady Holford's sister)

'Dining' probably meant a daytime meal, rather than an evening one, to take advantage of the best of the daylight and to avoid travelling further after dark. It is therefore likely that Queen Anne broke her journey here for lunch.

Right **Queen Anne;** painting by Sir Godfrey Kneller, c.1705 (Petworth)

The Williamsons

Anne Williamson was married to a professional soldier, Adam Williamson, but soon after they inherited Avebury Manor, he was appointed Lieutenant-Governor and Garrison Commander of Jamaica. Adam Williamson set out alone for the Caribbean, and greatly missed his wife, writing anxiously, 'I hope and trust I may be blessed with seeing you arrive in health and spirits'. Anne joined him in October 1791 and he became Governor the following month. However, she died, aged 47, in September 1794, probably of yellow fever, and was buried in St Catherine's Cathedral, Spanish Town.

Sir Adam was briefly Governor General of the British parts of San Domingo after he had been replaced as Governor of Jamaica. He returned alone to England in 1796 and remained a widower until his death on 21 October 1798. Despite a military career spanning 45 years spent in many hazardous spots, his demise followed a fall, in his own home, at Avebury Manor.

Right Sir Adam Williamson; miniature portrait painted by George Engleheart

Freedom and £5 a year

Following Sir Adam's death, an inventory of Avebury was compiled, providing a fascinating account of the contents of the house. In his will, Sir Adam granted his freedom, £5 and an annuity of £5 for life, to 'Sam my Mulatto boy', a slave he had brought back from Jamaica. 'Samuel Avebury', aged about 17, was baptised in December 1798, about six weeks after Sir Adam's death. It appears that he was not the only black person at the manor: Elizabeth Pearce, described as 'a Black formally a Servant in the ffamily [*sic*], was at the manor while the Williamsons were in Jamaica. 'Black Betty', as she was known, was left £10 and an annuity of £20 a year for life when Sir Adam died.

The Kemms

The Jenners

In 1816, after William and Jane Kemm won a lottery prize of £2,500 (the equivalent of around £90,000 today), they took out a lease on Avebury Manor and its surrounding farmland. For decades the Kemms paid rent to the Jones family, who had inherited the manor from Sir Adam Williamson. The tenancy continued after 1873, when Avebury was sold to the brewer and politician Sir Henry Meux.

To the Kemms, Avebury Manor was their business as well as the family home. Like all farmers, they had good years and bad. Two of their sons became clergymen, and Thomas Kemm's daughters taught local children to read and write in the Avebury National School. Thomas died in 1899 at the age of 83 and was buried in the churchyard of St James at Avebury.

Avebury in 1901
According to the census of 1901 Avebury Manor was inhabited only by two 'lady farmers', Marion Kemm (aged 46) and Everdell Kemm (aged 44). They employed a housemaid, aged 18, and a 15-year-old kitchenmaid. In 1902 the Kemms gave up the tenancy, and the contents of the manor, undisturbed for a century, were sold in a two-day auction. The catalogue echoes the 1798 inventory: an 'Early English' oak refectory table sold for sixteen guineas, and some 'fine old pewter plate' was snapped up.

In 1902 Avebury Manor was let by the Meux family to Colonel Leopold Jenner and his wife, Nora. Leopold's brother Walter was married to Nora's sister Flora, and the two couples shared a passion for old houses and gardens. In 1907 Leopold and Nora bought Avebury Manor, while Walter and Flora bought Lytes Cary in Somerset. Both buildings are now in the care of the National Trust.

The Avebury Jenners devoted the following two decades to restoring their home. One wall in the Tudor Parlour had to be rebuilt, which took two years. The Elizabethan chimneypiece had been consigned in pieces to an outhouse; it was repaired and reinstalled. Proponents of architectural salvage, they bought old oak panelling and installed it in the Tudor Parlour and the Tudor Bedchamber. Nora was a highly accomplished needlewoman and embroidered fine hangings for a replica eighteenth-century bed they commissioned from a local carpenter.

When the Great War broke out, Leopold rejoined the army. In the 1920s the couple built a new extension, the West Library (now the Tea-room), in a sympathetic style, and continued to create beautiful gardens around the house.

In 1929, the year of the Wall Street Crash, financial problems forced the Jenners to move to Bath and let their beloved house to the Benson family; eventually they were forced to

It has been said of the Jenners that they and Avebury Manor were perfectly suited to each other…they left Avebury Manor what it is today – a home where taste has been blended with comfort and tradition.

Sir Francis Knowles, a later owner of Avebury Manor

Leonard Jenner

Right The Jenners' joint gravestone in Avebury churchyard

sell it. They were so fond of Avebury, however, that they chose to be buried here, where their joint gravestone can still be seen in an area taken out of the manor garden and consecrated as part of the churchyard.

The romance of the past
In 1921 Avebury featured in the pages of *Country Life* magazine, which had done much to encourage the fashion for restoring ancient manor houses and furnishing them with suitably mellow antiques. Other examples now in the care of the National Trust include Westwood Manor in Wiltshire and Lytes Cary in Somerset.

Keiller and after

Alexander Keiller (1889–1950) bought Avebury Manor in 1937 to use as a base for his large-scale archaeological investigations on the 950 acres (384 hectares) he already owned around the house. He reinstated much of the largest stone circle in Europe, and he founded a museum to house his finds at Avebury.

Orphaned by the age of eighteen, Alexander Keiller had inherited a fortune from the firm of James Keiller & Sons of Dundee, most famous for its marmalade. He pursued many interests, including motor cars, skiing and flying, and he was married four times. He admired sixteenth- and seventeenth-century furniture and collected authentic pieces for the manor, although he grumbled that his private rooms were 'equipped with that indescribable degree of personal discomfort which can only come from exclusively period furniture of the middle of the sixteenth century'.

The Second World War curtailed Keiller's archaeological activities. In 1943 he sold most of his land around Avebury, including the stone circle, to the National Trust for £12,000. He also offered to sell the manor to the charity, but the National Trust declined. In 1955, shortly before his death, Keiller sold the house to Sir Francis Knowles.

Throughout the twentieth century, Avebury Manor was saved a number of times from dereliction by a succession of dedicated people – Leopold and Nora Jenner, Alexander

Above Keiller sketching on the Avebury excavation in 1934; a pencil drawing by his third wife, Doris Chapman (National Portrait Gallery)

Left Keiller's 1914 Malvern Torpedo Tourer

Below Keiller's fortune came from Dundee marmalade

GRAND MEDAL OF MERIT VIENNA 1873
JAMES KEILLER & SONS
DUNDEE
MARMALADE
ONLY PRIZE MEDAL FOR MARMALADE
LONDON . 1862

MEDAL OF MERIT VIENNA 1873
JAMES KEILLER & SONS
DUNDEE
MARMALADE
PRIZE MEDAL FOR MARMALADE
LONDON . 1862

I wanted a home for my family, and I loved Avebury Manor: and so at a time when most sensible people are moving out of places like Avebury, I moved in, for I did not feel that a place like this should die. I feel that the Dunches, Mervyns, Stawells, Holfords and thousands of others who have known Avebury would share this view.

Sir Francis Knowles

and Doris Keiller, and Sir Francis and Lady Knowles in particular – who appreciated its beauty and were able to ensure its survival. In 1976, Sir Francis's widow sold Avebury Manor to Michael Brudenell-Bruce, 8th Marquess of Ailesbury, and in 1981 it was sold to Mr and Mrs Nevill-Glidden. In 1988, entrepreneur Kenneth King bought the manor house for about £1 million, and announced plans to turn it into a Tudor-themed visitor attraction, which caused local controversy. In 1991, following Mr King's bankruptcy, the manor was sold to the National Trust by the Official Receivers. It was leased to private tenants, who opened parts of the house on behalf of the National Trust, until 2009. We subsequently opened more of the house, showing it largely empty and telling the stories of some of the families who had lived here.

Left Sir Francis and Lady Knowles with their children in the Tudor Parlour in 1956. They were the first owners of Avebury Manor to open it to the public

The Exterior

Avebury Manor is built of local grey sandstone, known as sarsen, and has evolved over many centuries. Successive owners added various extensions and improvements, a patchwork of gables, mullioned windows and chimneys, creating an idiosyncratic but attractive house.

In 2011 the National Trust commissioned a full historic building survey of the manor. Primary documentary sources on the house were unusually scarce, but Wessex Archaeology Limited turned up crucial new evidence. An oak beam in the Kitchen was analysed using dendrochronology (tree-ring dating), revealing a felling date of between 1555 and 1580. This is the earliest dated evidence for the manor; as the property was bought in the 1550s by William Dunch, it is possible that this date reflects his building or rebuilding of the manor. A south-facing wing was added by Sir James and Lady Mervyn around 1600, providing a Great Hall (now the Dining Room) with the Great Chamber (now the Queen Anne Bedchamber) above. It is likely that the Mervyns also commissioned the Tudor Parlour and Tudor Bedchamber at the same time; both have fine plasterwork ceilings. A detailed plan of 1695 (see inside front cover) provides a comprehensive map of the house and grounds. A sketch from the 1720s by the antiquary William Stukeley established that the original roofline must have been altered later, probably in the 1740s, when Richard Holford extensively remodelled the south front, modernising the Great Hall and turning it into a dining room in the contemporary classical style. He also substantially modified the chamber above, creating a magnificent coved ceiling in the opened-up roof space. This was only possible because he had removed gables along the south front. Indeed, the discovery of invoices for a large quantity of roofing materials confirms that these major works were undertaken in 1740–41.

For most of the nineteenth century, Avebury Manor was tenanted by the Kemms, a family of farmers, and little new structural work was undertaken. By the time ownership passed to the Jenners in 1907, the fabric of the building was in great need of repair. They restored the house and garden, reinstated forgotten elements such as the magnificent fireplace in the Tudor Parlour, acquired authentic panelling through architectural salvage, converted an unused area into what is now the Billiard Room, installed central heating, and built an impressive library on the west side, which blends seamlessly with the far older structure. This was the last major alteration to the 'footprint' of the house; subsequent owners have maintained the fabric of the building sympathetically.

Left The south-east corner

The Tudor Parlour

This attractive room is presented to reflect the prestige and social status of William Dunch, a prosperous Tudor courtier, who built the first wing of Avebury Manor, probably in the 1550s. There are stone-mullioned and transomed windows on three walls, allowing in the maximum amount of daylight. The oak wainscoting is authentically sixteenth- or seventeenth-century, but wasn't installed here until the early twentieth century. The Jenners also reinstated the original fireplace, which dates from around 1600 and was found in pieces in an outhouse.

Ceiling
The fine plaster ceiling of geometric motifs dates from around 1600. The sophisticated pattern of interlocking lozenges was copied by the Jenners in the 1920s in their design for the topiary garden.

Tapestries
An Elizabethan country gentleman's house would have had panels of hanging textiles such as tapestries on the walls of the principal rooms, both as an indication of their owner's wealth and cultural sophistication and as a practical form of insulation. For the 2011 project, designer Russell Sage commissioned photographic copies of the Abraham Tapestries in the Great Hall at Hampton Court, which had been acquired by Henry VIII and are now cared for by Historic Royal Palaces. The images were meticulously printed on linen panels by the firm of Zardi and Zardi.

Furniture
The oak furniture, including the elegant armchairs (his and hers), was newly-made by Guy Butcher based on historic designs. The date of 1547 on the larger chair is significant because that is the year of the Dunches' marriage; it is also the year in which Avebury Manor became private property after centuries of ownership by the Church and then the Crown. To modern eyes it is surprising to see how light-coloured oak is when new. Other furniture includes an aumbry (a food cupboard), a joined table and four stools for lower-status members of the household.

Floor
Rush matting was extensively used in the Tudor era as it was soft, resilient and sound-muffling, with a pleasant, fresh smell. The flooring in this room was handwoven by Rush Matters, using English bulrushes.

Right **The Tudor Parlour**

Pride in arms

The heraldic panel over the fireplace is a modern creation, executed by Grant Watt, in emulation of heraldic painted decoration from the 1580s at Canons Ashby in Northamptonshire. Specialist advice was sought from the College of Arms, and it incorporates elements from the Dunch coat of arms. Coming from humble origins, William Dunch is likely to have been very proud of his coat of arms, and would have been keen to have it displayed.

The Tudor Bedchamber

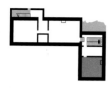

Right The plasterwork ceiling in the Tudor Bedchamber

Below The carved chalk fireplace in the Tudor Bedchamber

Opposite The Tudor Bedchamber

This room is styled to represent the marriage in the late 1590s of William Dunch's widowed daughter-in-law, Deborah, to the wealthy landowner Sir James Mervyn.

Ceiling

Elements of the ornate geometric plasterwork ceiling and the moulded frieze above the wainscoting have been picked out in bold colours; paint analysis wasn't able to establish whether there had been any colour here originally, but it was a technique used in similar interiors, such as at Plas Mawr in Wales, so it was introduced here for decorative effect. The motifs on the ceiling have significant attributes; the peacock symbolises immortality in the lexicon of Tudor iconography, the lion bravery and strength, and the unicorn purity.

Sleep tight

The bed incorporates a substantially renovated seventeenth-century frame, with carved wooden posts, a modern cornice and a tester (top) added by the Four Poster Bed Company. The frame has holes bored at regular intervals to support a horizontal lattice of ropes which needed regularly tightening – hence the archaic phrase, 'night, night, sleep tight'. The bed has three mattresses (straw, wool with horsehair, and duck down) and bolsters and pillows, all covered with ticking (so-called because its tight weave deters the passage of parasites). There is even a woollen blanket, Tudor Wiltshire having been renowned for its wool.

The bed-hangings and textiles were designed and made by Master-weaver Ian Dale of Angus Weavers of Brechin in Scotland, using the vast archives in the Victoria & Albert Museum for research. A heavy linen twill (known as 'say') was handwoven from lustrous Flemish flax for the bed-hangings and tester pelmet. The coverlet is decorated with embroidered 'slips', appliquéd embroideries based on the 'eye' from a peacock's tail feathers, made by the Royal School of Needlework and stitched to the coverlet by skilled volunteers. Underneath the four-poster is a truckle bed, with its simple wooden frame and short legs, providing a functional berth for a servant or child.

Fireplace

The large fireplace of carved chalk dates from around 1600. The chimneypiece was limewashed as part of the 2011 project, as it would have been in the past, and a fireback was specially made, combining the initials of Deborah and James Mervyn (the 'J' being represented as an 'I', as was common at the time), to match the couple's initials over the front porch.

The Queen Anne Bedchamber

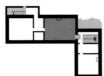

Well-connected Sir Richard Holford bought Avebury Manor in 1694. He may have entertained Queen Anne at the manor in the early 1700s as a servant's account of 1712 relates that she was said to have dined here. It is possible that this was in 1703, when she visited Bath to take the waters for her health. In that era, courtiers would arrange brief stops at superior houses, so that their monarch could 'retire' in privacy, and dine, if necessary.

The architectural decoration of the room and the creation of the high coved ceiling were always considered to be later in date than this. During the BBC project, buildings archaeologists from Wessex Archaeology discovered documentary evidence which indicated that the roof was substantially remodelled around 1740 by Sir Richard's grandson, another Richard, in keeping with contemporary fashion.

Painted decoration

The decorative scheme created in 2011 draws on historic examples, such as Het Loo Palace, in the Netherlands, and the Balcony Room of the 1690s at nearby Dyrham Park. Advised by Russell Sage and Dan Cruickshank, specialist painters Grant Watt and Corin Sands combined a dark red porphyry colour with orange-pink in imitation of Siena marble, as the background on the walls. The coving was painted as *trompe-l'oeil* clouds – grand ceilings of this era often implied a heavenly vista – and opulent touches of gilding were added to the cornicing.

Left The coved ceiling has been painted with illusionistic clouds

Right The Queen Anne Bedchamber

Opposite The Avebury bed was inspired by the State Bed of about 1704 at Dyrham Park

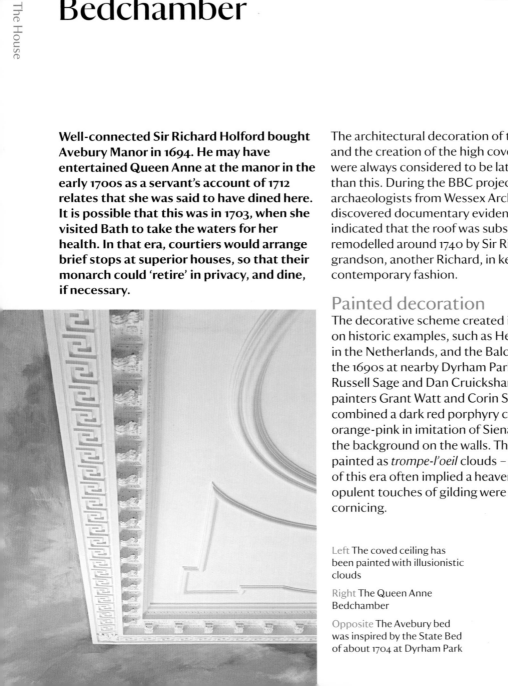

State Bed

The design of the bed drew on the State Bed of about 1704 at Dyrham, and other examples in the Victoria & Albert Museum. The frame incorporated two pairs of slightly later bed-posts. A domed tester seemed appropriate for this room, and the bed was fitted with a complex moulded cornice made in sections. The opulent hangings and curtains, in rich red and gold, were woven by the Gainsborough Silk Weaving Company with historically accurate silk damask. The bed is furnished with layers of mattresses and white silk sheets. Ornate urn-shaped 'Avebury Tassels' were designed by Russell Sage and made as finials for the four-poster by Henry Newbery, a firm established in 1782.

Appropriate hand-carved furniture was recreated by ELG at Jonathan Sainsbury Ltd, based on examples at Dyrham, and upholstered with silk damask to match the bed. All the furniture was made from solid walnut. The portrait of Queen Anne was created by Thomasina Smith, drawing on the famous triple portrait of Charles I, by Van Dyck; multiple portraits were not uncommon in the seventeenth and eighteenth centuries, as a preparation for sculpture.

The Queen Anne Ante-chamber
The Withdrawing Room
The Closet

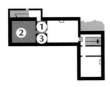

1 The Queen Anne Ante-chamber

The Oriental-style room next to the Queen Anne Bedchamber is shown as if it was an ante-chamber to the Withdrawing Room beyond. The fashion for chinoiserie was a fascinating counter-current to eighteenth-century Britain's fixation on classicism.

Authentic Chinese wallpapers were expensive and often difficult to procure, so enterprising London 'paper-stainers' produced wallpapers in imitation of Chinese imports. One example survives in the Victoria & Albert Museum, a woodblock print of about 1700, to which colour stencilling and a coat of varnish were added, mimicking the texture of lacquer. Inspired by the V & A's 'oriental' wallpaper, specialist painter Mark Sands created a large-scale stencil to cover the walls of the Ante-chamber. He hand-painted the chinoiserie design, but included witty and subtle references to the Wiltshire countryside, such as wild pansies, butterflies, great crested newts and a fox, as well as some of the Avebury stones. In Keiller's time there was a real hand-painted Chinese wallpaper here.

Right The chinoiserie decoration in the Queen Anne Ante-chamber has been handpainted by Mark Sands over a stencilled and chalked outline

Above right **The Withdrawing Room**

Below right **The close stool in the Closet**

Painting
The painting is based on a picture in the Royal Collection, believed to have been bought by Queen Anne. It reflects the growing fascination with exotic birds and beasts as British explorers and merchants travelled further afield. Artist Corin Sands re-interpreted this image in acrylic paint on canvas.

3 The Closet
Next to the Withdrawing Room is the Closet, which was intended as a 'place of easement' for the monarch. It contains a 'close stool' a portable loo, embroidered by members of the Marlborough Embroiders Guild. In an era before plumbing, this was an essential part of the monarch's travelling equipment.

2 The Withdrawing Room
A withdrawing room was where a visiting Queen would be attended by her closest servants and entertained by her favourites. The Jenners fitted dark wooden wainscoting in the early twentieth century, but the elegant fireplace dates from around 1700.

Day-bed
The day-bed was specially made of solid walnut by ELG at Jonathan Sainsbury Ltd, and inspired by an example at Dyrham, but wider; Queen Anne was obese, and stout furniture was needed to support her weight. High-backed chairs, with horsehair padding and appropriate upholstery, were also made to accommodate visitors. The silk and damask textiles for this room were handwoven by the Gainsborough Silk Weaving Company. Sumptuous ruched curtains and ornate pelmets were added to the windows, and matching fabric panels were mounted over wooden battens to line the walls, creating a more regal and feminine decorative scheme.

The Governor of Jamaica's Dining Room

The Dining Room was built around 1600, with a front door leading straight into the room. Around 1740, a dividing wall was built to create a separate entrance hall, and the room was redecorated in the Palladian style, with carved classical pediments above the symmetrically arranged doors.

Wallpaper

The 2011 design team wanted to reflect the career and extensive travels of Sir Adam Williamson, a former soldier and Governor of Jamaica. By the late eighteenth century there was a passion for Chinese imports, especially wallpapers. This hand-painted paper was supplied by Fromental and made in Wuxi in China specially to fit this room. It is in the tradition of 'narrative' papers popular during Sir Adam's lifetime. The panoramic scenes depict British trade with China in tea and ceramics, while the West Indies are represented by islands dotted with palm trees. Each of the 22 panels was hand-painted in gouache, and hung using a traditional starch-based glue.

Furniture

The 2011 design team drew on the comprehensive inventory compiled after Sir Adam's death in 1798. The dining table is the focal point of the room, and Sir Adam dined here in some luxury, even when alone, but especially when his nieces and other guests visited. Candlelight from tall candelabras was the usual form of illumination in wealthy houses in this era, and table silver added to the lustre of the evening meal; the eighteenth-century-style glasses were made for the *Manor Reborn* project by Emsie Sharp. The exercise chair is modelled on one which belonged to John Wesley, the founder of Methodism. 'Chamber horses' imitated the movement of a cantering horse and provided a vigorous form of exercise during inclement weather. Sir Adam's chamber horse appears in the 1798 inventory, although his was kept on the 'best staircase'. This model was constructed by modern craftsmen working for ELG at Jonathan Sainsbury Ltd, using reclaimed Georgian mahogany.

The sofa is also new, made by furniture makers George Smith in the style of a 1780s piece by Hepplewhite, and upholstered with silk and cotton damask to match the dining chairs.

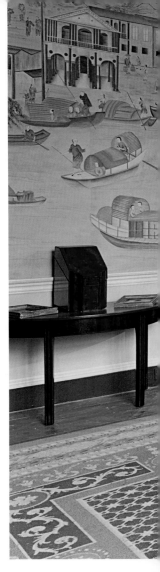

Left Avebury Manor features in the Chinese wallpaper in the Governor of Jamaica's Dining Room

Above The Governor of Jamaica's Dining Room

Carpet and curtains

There was a large Wilton carpet in this room in the 1798 inventory, so Ulster Carpets were commissioned to design an appropriate and unique piece in the classical style, based on historical records. There were also green curtains mentioned in the inventory, so a magnificent design by Thomas Sheraton for the Prince of Wales's Chinese Drawing Room at Carlton House in London was copied.

Painting

Above the fireplace is a painting in eighteenth-century style, by Corin Sands, of the Governor's official residence in Spanish Town, the former capital of Jamaica where the Williamsons once lived.

The Kitchen

The Kitchen and the Keiller Parlour next door are the oldest parts of the house; the ceiling beam above the fireplace comes from a tree felled between 1555 and 1580. The kitchen was the 'engine room' of Avebury Manor over the centuries, the source of food, hot water, deliveries, news and gossip. Next door was the servants' hall, in a wing of the house added in 1750, where the staff ate and spent any leisure time, or tackled 'clean' domestic tasks such as mending.

The Kitchen is presented as it could have looked in 1912, when the house was owned by the Jenners. Surviving photographs of the room helped to inform the 2011 design team. It is evident that the servants' daily life was very labour-intensive, despite the gadgets and grinders, mincers and tools, scales, carpet-beaters and spice-boxes. Endless piles of dirty dishes needed to be laboriously washed by hand, in an era before rubber gloves or effective detergents. The sinks and wooden work surfaces required vigorous scrubbing daily with hot water and sand.

The central table was where most of the food preparation took place. The magnificent wooden dresser was painted blue during the *Manor Reborn* project, a colour often used in the past because it was popularly believed to deter flies. It was a useful place to store and display ceramic plates and dishes; the cupboards below contain kitchen implements. A barrel-backed eighteenth-century cupboard

– very similar to one at Lytes Cary, owned by the Jenners' relatives – pre-dates the project and was already set at right-angles to the wall, probably to protect anyone sitting on the bench from draughts when the door was opened.

The typical Victorian or Edwardian cast-iron range was easier to regulate than an open fire, and provided ample hot water for domestic use, but it needed blackleading every morning and could consume a ton of coal a month. For this kitchen, architectural salvage expert Neville Griffin found an authentic Wellstood range dating from about 1904, in a house in the Wirral which was about to be demolished. The range was restored and installed as the centrepiece of this atmospheric and cosy room.

The servants in 1911
According to the 1911 census, there were six resident servants working in the house, all women. The cook, Mrs Lena Bevan, was a widow from Somerset in her forties, and she relied on a young kitchenmaid, Edith Bessie Porter. The two housemaids, Agnes Hancock and Agnes Kimmer, were recruited locally; there was a parlourmaid, Jane Nash, and Mrs Jenner had a 43-year-old lady's maid, Miss Rosam. It is likely they also employed a manservant, but he did not appear on the census for the night of 2 April 1911, which implies that he 'lived out'.

Left The Kitchen

Opposite A Wellstood cast-iron range was restored and installed in the Kitchen

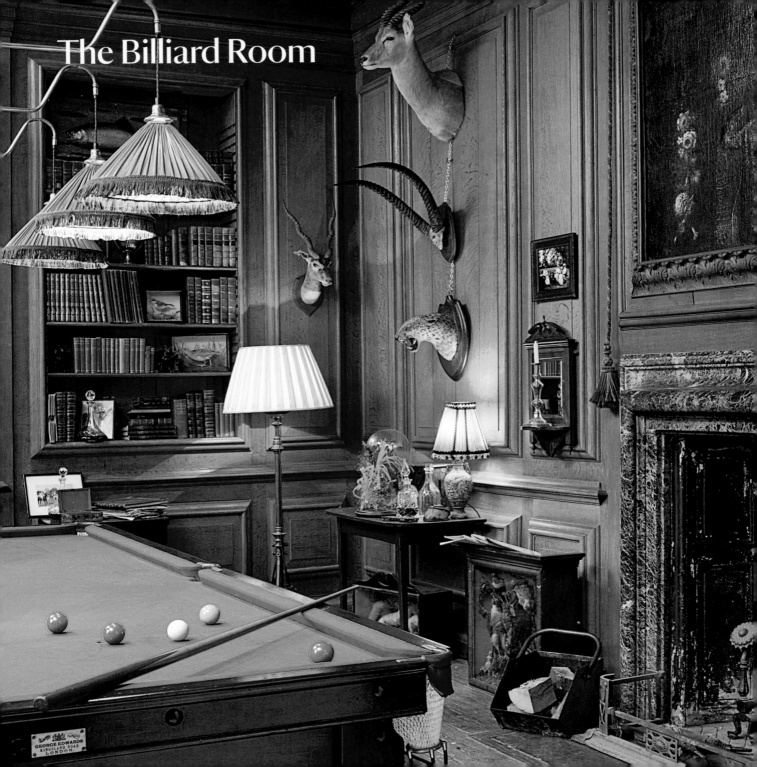

The Billiard Room

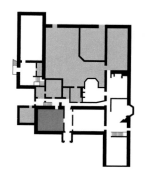

This room was built around 1600 as part of the extension carried out by the Mervyns, but it was depicted as two modest rooms – a 'pantry' and an 'inner cellar' – on the 1695 plan. It may even have had a very low ceiling to accommodate a middle floor lit by windows that are still visible from outside. When the Jenners arrived in 1902, they described the space as 'unfloored, disused, almost ruinous', so they completely remodelled it between 1907 and 1920, transforming a neglected corner into a library worthy of Sir Richard Holford, the owner in 1700. They commissioned a local carpenter to make wooden panelling, and introduced a handsome maroon and green Cornish Serpentine marble fireplace with deeply curved carving, known as bolection moulding. The two paintings introduced by them were investigated as a part of the *Manor Reborn* project and were identified by the National Trust's painting specialist as by a little-known French painter of the seventeenth century, Jacques Hupin. Very few paintings are known by this artist and only one other is in a public collection.

In 2011, Russell Sage wanted to reflect the masculine ambience of a country gentleman's 'den' in the years after the First World War. Leopold Jenner had been a professional soldier, and he rejoined the army at the advanced age of 45 in 1914, surviving campaigns in Egypt, Gallipoli and France. His career was successful and he was promoted to Lieutenant-Colonel. A consummate sportsman in his youth, Leopold had excelled at polo, representing England against Ireland in 1907. He was skilled at fencing and a keen huntsman, so sporting memorabilia, hunting trophies and military mementoes were also sourced.

The three-quarter-size six-legged mahogany billiard table dominating the room dates from around 1900, and was restored by the specialist firm, Hubble Sports.

The baize-covered table has a five-piece Welsh slate bed and weighs 1200 kgs (1.2 tons). Billiards was a game which was mostly played by men, and well-appointed country houses of the Victorian and Edwardian eras often had a billiard room as a masculine retreat and a place where they could smoke. The table is set up for snooker, as that game is now better known. You are encouraged to have a go.

This atmospheric room uses contemporary music and periodicals, and a whiff of (synthetic) cigar smoke, to evoke the sense of a gentleman's room designed for leisure and pleasure around 1919. In selecting appropriate furniture and artefacts, Russell looked for rather worn but good quality 'country house pieces' typical of those owned by the rural gentry.

Opposite The Billiard Room

Below The polo mallets in the Billiard Room recall that Leopold Jenner was a polo player of international standard

The Keiller Parlour

This low-ceilinged room is in the oldest part of the house, dating from the 1550s. By 1695 it had been subdivided into a very small parlour, with a chimney across one corner, a larder next door, an entrance passage and a passage to the Kitchen. A small staircase twisted upwards close to the entrance. The present chimneypiece and bow window were probably added in the eighteenth century. The Jenners opened up the room, removing the dividing walls, in the early twentieth century.

'I have to tell you now …'

This room celebrates the life, times and varied interests of Alexander Keiller, although it reflects contemporary interiors which he would have known elsewhere rather than being a re-creation of the room as it was in his time. Between 1925 and 1929, Keiller organised excavations at nearby Windmill Hill, moving on to the stone circles and avenue at Avebury between 1934 and 1939. He rented Avebury Manor, and then bought it in 1937. This room is presented as though it was Sunday morning, 3 September 1939, with radio recordings of dance music and the official BBC broadcast of the declaration of war bringing a chill to this peaceful haven. Two days before, Doris and Alexander Keiller had welcomed some of the 70 East End children and their five teachers who had been evacuated to Avebury.

Above **The Keiller Parlour**

Left **The zebra chair in the Keiller Parlour**

Opposite **The folding screen in the Keiller Parlour**

Screen, curtains and cushions

The artist Mark Sands was inspired by a 1920s decorative frieze originally designed for the Derry and Toms department store, which is now in the Victoria & Albert Museum. He made and painted a subtle Art Deco-style, four-panel folding screen to act as a room divider. Mark's brother, Corin Sands, painted an interpretation of Paul Nash's colour lithograph of *Landscape with Megaliths*, dating from 1937. Nash had been fascinated by the enigmatic standing stones of Avebury, first visiting in 1933. The damask fabric for the curtains and window-seat cushions was specially woven by the Gainsborough Silk Weaving Company, and its 1930s-style design reveals Modernist and Cubist influences.

The carpet was specially made by Ulster Carpets, and the abstract Art Deco-style design reflects Keiller's lifelong passion for motor cars; one of his favourites, a rare 1914 20hp Malvern Torpedo Tourer with a 4-cylinder 4060cc engine, made by Sizaire Berwick, was purchased by the National Trust and is on show in the Great Barn. It was customised by Keiller so that the front seats convert into a double bed.

The Gardens

The West Library (Tea-room)

Below The West Library

The West Library, with its stone-tiled roof and sarsen walls, and the linking lobby and staircase, were built as a harmonious extension to the manor by the Jenners around 1920. It was painted the current deep blue-green about 1990. This elegant room, lined with bookshelves and second-hand books for sale, is now a popular tea-room, serving food and beverages in vintage crockery. An external flight of steps runs from the lobby door to the formal Topiary Garden below.

The Walled Gardens

Influenced by Arts and Crafts Movement practitioners such as Gertrude Jekyll, Leopold and Nora Jenner created a sequence of delightful walled gardens at Avebury Manor, their shapes designed to follow the remains of old hedges and walls; the curving half-moon brick wall is believed to date back to the early eighteenth century.

Immediately outside the West Library, the Topiary Garden, created entirely by the Jenners, has huge sculptural shapes in yew disposed around a rectangular pool with waterlilies, a haven for wildlife. The geometric design of interlocking lozenges in box was copied from the ceiling of the Tudor Parlour.

All of the high-walled gardens are very warm and sheltered, protected from the ravages of wind, and make an ideal setting for espaliered fruit trees. The sunny brick walls also support elderly vines and honeysuckle, with pansies and borage to attract bees. There is a strong sculptural sense to the grounds;

well-worn flagstones provide paths between matching pairs of massive yews, whose looming forms subtly echo the shapes of the sarsens in the nearby Avenue. The orchard is surrounded by well-shaped yew hedges, while the south lawn features an astrolabe mounted on an elaborate pedestal. One poignant feature in the garden is the pet cemetery, containing small gravestones from the time of the Jenners and later.

Above **The West Library (left) and the Topiary Garden**

Right **The pet cemetery**

The Kitchen Garden

The walled Kitchen Garden was designed in 2011 by David Howard, formerly Head Gardener at Highgrove to HRH the Prince of Wales. 40 local volunteers cleared the waist-high scrub and bushes which had overgrown the neglected site. They built raised beds, a potting shed, and a Victorian-style glasshouse. Subsequently the National Trust added a heated propagating bench for seedlings in the glasshouse, cold frames for hardening off delicate plants, and fruit cages to protect soft fruit.

The traditional kitchen garden supplied fresh fruit and vegetables, herbs and cut flowers, for the 'big house' throughout the year. The Avebury Manor garden team now grows onions, garlic, shallots, parsnips, beetroot, celeriac, potatoes and runner beans. Along the sunny wall by the Racquets Court, there are fan-trained greengages and plums, while running the length of the garden is an avenue of espaliered pear trees, planted and maintained by the National Trust staff. The cut-flower beds provide seasonal blooms such as sweet peas and chrysanthemums for use in the house.

While the glasshouse was being erected, two squatters were discovered – great crested newts. *Titurus cristatus* is a European Protected Species, so these rare creatures were provided with a secure custom-built property of their own near the compost bins, promptly nicknamed Newt Manor. Painter Mark Sands even incorporated a picture of the Avebury Manor amphibians in his Chinese-style wall-painting in the Queen Anne Ante-chamber.

Below The newly restored Kitchen Garden

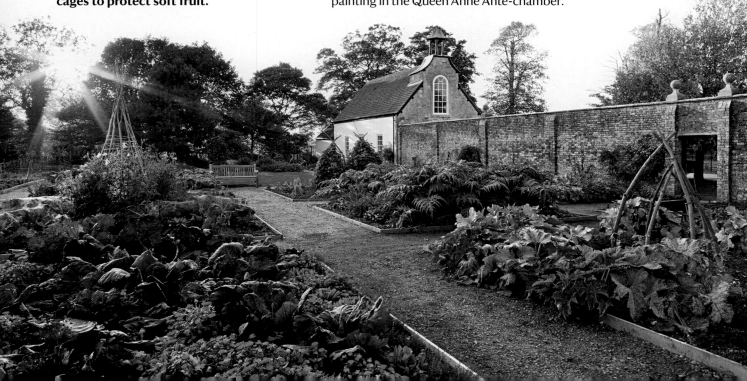